Central Australia

1927

John Flynn

AF585081

ETT IMPRINT
Exile Bay

First published in Imprint Classics by ETT Imprint, Exile Bay 2026

First published by *The Inlander* as No. 19 in October 1927

First electronic edition ETT Imprint 2026

This edition copyright © ETT Imprint 2026

This book is copyright. A part from any fair dealing for the purposes of private study, research criticism or review, as permitted under the Copyright Act, no par may be reproduced by any process without written permission. Inquiries should be addressed to the publishers or by email to ettimprint@hotmail.com:

ETT IMPRINT
PO Box R1906
Royal Exchange NSW 1225 Australia

ISBN 978-1-923527-05-8 (paper)

ISBN 978-1-923527-06-5 (ebook)

Cover and design by Tom Thompson

The Inlander

A VOICE FROM THE UTTERMOST FRONTIERS
OF SETTLEMENT IN AUSTRALIA

PUBLISHED BY THE A.I.M. BOARD
TO STIMULATE
THE BATTLE FOR A BRIGHTER BUSH

EDITED BY REV. JOHN FLYNN
INLAND SUPERINTENDENT, PRESBYTERIAN CHURCH OF AUSTRALIA
(Whose home is "The Wallaby," and whose postal address is
Box 100, G.P.O., Sydney.)

NUMBER 19
(OCTOBER, 1927)

Like other Bush Travellers, "The Inlander" appears as best it can!

To Members of The Inland Legion, "The Inlander" is sent out from Headquarters on the inclusive plan. Persons who do not desire to subscribe to the A.I.M. may obtain copies through their Booksellers.

PRICE: ONE SHILLING
Postal Rate is: "Printed Matter 1d. for four ozs."

Wholesale Agents—GORDON & GOTCH (Australasia), Ltd.

Printed in Australia by Jackson, O'Sullivan & Mortlock Ltd.,
276-282 Devonshire Street, Sydney.

1927

PALM VALLEY, CENTRAL AUSTRALIA.
Now a National Reserve. Young palms are growing freely.

CENTRAL AUSTRALIA.

This year, after long use merely as a popular term, "Central Australia" has been elevated to official recognition; it now denotes a section of what was formerly "Northern Territory," comprising all of the old territory lying south of the 20th parallel. That portion left to north is now officially known as "North Australia." (See map at end of volume.)

The change is welcome and useful. But one cannot help regretting our national timidity on the sea of terms. "Australia," "North Australia," "Central Australia," "South Australia," "Western Australia," all now on the map; why not be consistent and substitute for Queensland, New South Wales, Victoria and Tasmania the respective titles of "North-east Australia," "Eastern Australia," "South-east Australia," and "Little Australia"!!!

If lacking this courage of consistency, we might respond to the promptings of increasing national consciousness by restricting the use of our noble name, "Australia," absolutely to Commonwealth affairs. We could then give real, instead of patchwork, names to the present four sub-Australias, and complete the task by finding another one-piece title for our southern reminder of Wales.

It is fitting that, at the very moment of Central Australia's birth as a separate entity, attention of the public generally throughout the Continent should be turning thereto in quite a new way. During the last two years the number of visitors has run into hundreds. With the railway, a regular tourist traffic will develop.

As to progress of the extension from Oodnadatta: An instalment is already completed, by day labour, to a point 21 miles north of Oodnadatta, where large quantities of rails, sleepers, etc., are already being assembled for future use, under an arrangement by which the Commonwealth Works and Railways Department is providing all materials. The contract to construct the line (labour only) at a price of £695,320 has been let to "Victorian Construction Pty. Ltd." for the remaining 271 miles, work to proceed immediately. The estimate of total cost is £1,700,000, and the date for completion is 30th June, 1929.

WHAT OODNADATTA SEES IN BAD DREAMS!
(All that is left of Warrina, 45 miles south—a busy township before the railhead was moved on.)

In passing, it may be mentioned that arrangements are being made for a "Welfare Missionary" to serve among the men on construction work, under a co-operative plan in which various churches and societies will be associated with the A.I.M.

Meantime, the Darwin-Katherine line is being steadily extended, and will soon reach Daly Waters. Thus, until the next burst of activity, there will remain a gap of a little more than 550 miles, over which a good motor track can be made for slight cost. We understand that a fleet of fast motor cars is contemplated, making possible a fairly satisfactory north-south transcontinental passenger traffic.

As already intimated in the public press, there will soon be a regular aerial passenger service between Daly Waters and Brisbane, giving the camels one more nasty jar!

How does one get to Central Australia now? Book from Adelaide to Oodnadatta for the fortnightly passenger train—frequent specials run, but are not recommended for comfort, and seem to be missing just when desired. Thursday morning, 7.15, is the time of departure, and a fast train follows the broad gauge (5ft. 3in. as in Victoria) to Terowie (138 miles—12.57 p.m.), where 21 minutes are allowed to transfer luggage to the narrow gauge (3ft. 6in., as in

Queensland). Those who know, slip across the overhead bridge to the refreshment room, where meals of excellent "home" quality are served.

Quorn (234 miles) is reached at 6.4 p.m. Here one has to transfer luggage to the "Far North" train (also 3ft. 6in. gauge), which boasts a sleeping car of somewhat cramped type, four to the cabin. The balance of 26 minutes is used to snatch an evening meal, or join the crowd assembled to speed the other train to Port Augusta, 25 miles south. Port Augusta-Oodnadatta line is already under management of the Commonwealth Railway Department.

During the night one passes through Hawker (275 miles), Beltana (353 miles), and thus reaches Marree (formerly "Hergott Springs," 441 miles) on Friday morning at 6.28. There is plenty of time to transfer luggage from the sleeping car to the day car, and stroll over to the hotel for breakfast before the last stage begins at 7.30.

Bopeechi siding is passed at 9.30, after which one should be on the lookout—to the right—for the very dreary, therefore interesting, shores of Lake Eyre. This large "dead sea" runs 120 miles to the north, 45 miles east to west; but only this one glimpse is obtainable from the train. Here the line is well below sea level, as far as Stuart's Creek siding, which itself is 3ft. below.

William Creek (566 miles, 251ft. above sea) is reached at 2.16 p.m., where a long break is allowed to replenish coal for the engine; passengers take the hint, and partake of a good homely meal at a house nearby.

At Algebuckina (653 miles, 6.20 p.m.) one of the longest bridges in Australia spans the Neale River, which runs a torrent once every ten years or so, and, in between, maintains one visible, good, permanent waterhole.

Oodnadatta (688 miles) is reached, officially speaking, at 7.57. A while back, during reconstruction of bridges and permanent way to carry heavy engines, the train crept in at any time between then and sunrise, but vagaries of that kind are now rare, except after a sandstorm has been busy.

Visitors who travel in their own motor cars have choice of routes from Adelaide. One runs via Gawler, Claire, Jamestown, Carrieton and Hawker, to Marree. A spare day to run out from Hawker to Wilpena Pound, in the heart of Flinders Ranges, is strongly recommended. The mountain scenery is unique around St. Mary's Peak, which rises to 4,800 ft.; and the "Pound," a vast natural paddock, ringed in by perpendicular hills except for the narrow gorge through which a solitary creek emerges, is something to write home about. It inspired the famous hiding place for stolen cattle, which is featured in our classic bushranging story, and before long will, doubtless, appear on the silver sheet.

From Parachilna siding (330 miles) a run into the hills, where a T.B. Sanatarium has recently been established, is well worth while. From Copley (formerly "Leigh's Creek," 373 miles) a most picturesque road runs out over 100 miles eastward to Paralana Springs, which have recently been making a bid for fame on account of their healing properties.

In good seasons experienced local motorists may make the journey from Marree to Oodnadatta in one day. But there are apt to be treacherous bogs and washouts after rains, and, in dry times, the track may be altogether ruined by sand-drifts. Casual visitors should always arrange their arrival at Marree to suit the train, and truck their cars from there to Oodnadatta.

An interesting alternative route from Adelaide runs through the rich, agricultural lands of Balaclava, thence via Red Hill, Port Pirie, and Port Germain, to Port Augusta —mostly along the future, shortened, route of the East-West transcontinental express—thence through the beautiful Pichi Richi Pass to Quorn, and on to Marree. Or one may turn north-west along the transcontinental railway to Kingoonya (209 miles) then north another 200 miles to Coober Pedy opal fields, and 110 miles to William Creek. This way offers little difficulty to mechanical motorists who carry pocket workshops with them; but, owing to big

How we motor from Marree to Oodnadatta!
(Six weary cars on this train.)

chances of mishaps, and remote chances of other cars passing by, we advise all others to keep to route of frequent traffic. One can obtain, while nearer home, all the marathon walks that health demands.

Oodnadatta is 396ft. above sea, and owes an inestimable debt to its bore, through which an ample supply of good water flows up from nearly 1,500 ft. below. Lawns and some flowers and vegetables are grown by some few enthusiasts, though garden beds have to be continually renewed owing to gradual impregnation from soda; but

STARTING OUT.
Mr. Chapman, of Blood's Creek, 100 miles north, uses car and trailer. Most folk prefer motor lorries for heavy duty.

THE PRIDE OF OODNADATTA.
Hookey's Hole, on the Neale River. Although the rainfall averages only 4½ inches, there is generally water here, as it lasts well over a year without replenishing.

trees and shrubs have provided easier reward to many, giving the township a restful air to one who has battled thither over barren tracks.

Wants of residents and visitors are catered for by post and telegraph office incorporated with the railway, school, police station, Soldiers' Memorial Hall, one well-stocked general store with garage attached, hotel (with a neat, detached bungalow for visitors), several boarding-houses, blacksmith's shop, carpenter, butcher and baker; an inspector of wells and bores lives here, also a band of missionaries to the aborigines.

There is also Dr. Shanahan (a railway official with private practice also), who serves—as opportunity offers—between here and Marree. Until the aeroplanes get busy in these parts, people off the line must take their chance.

To the A.I.M. Family the centre of interest at Oodnadatta is the Nursing Home ("The Hostel") and the Inland Club, the latter a side-line which has grown out of the general social service rendered by "The Hostel" when nurs-

Sister Sinclair escorting A.I.M. enthusiasts from Adelaide and Melbourne. Looking away from Hookey's Hole the landscape is not inviting, having for long years been "eaten out" around the water.

ing duties were not pressing. It is interesting to recall that the first nurse was stationed here by the Presbyterian Church of South Australia, through the "Smith of Dunesk" Committee, some time before Lady Dudley inspired the "Bush Nursing" movement, which is doing so much for settlers in the "betwixt and between" areas. Sister Main arrived about 1907, with the blessing of many who had been stirred to action by the Rev. Frank Rolland, M.C., then minister in these lands, now Principal of Geelong College. The Hostel—secretly and substantially assisted by the late Mr. and Mrs. R. Barr Smith, of Adelaide—was officially opened by Rev. R. Mitchell, who towered picturesquely above Sister Mary Bett while the thermometer played around 106 (at 8 p.m.!) in December of 1911. Rev. John Flynn, then minister for the Smith of Dunesk Mission, was clerk of works. Next year the A.I.M. was founded to carry forward and extend all sorts of good works for isolated areas of this unique continent; so, in 1913, The Hostel was transferred to the new all-States organisation.

Sisters Sinclair, MacNeil and Calderwood now find much to do since railway extension has brought so many

The Hostel. The Club.

A.I.M. BUILDINGS AT OODNADATTA.

more people about, and the building (now in final stages of gradual reconstruction and addition) is rendering service far beyond our early anticipations. The Inland Club is always open to the public, and every passer-by is welcome to use it for writing, reading, rest or games—not to

—Photo Edgar Horwood

AFTER THE RAINS.

On the sandy stretch south of Hamilton Bore, one far-flung mass of flowering herbage, etc. A few months before it was absolutely naked sand just here.

OPEN-AIR WARD AT THE HOSTEL.

(Also Resonian Evans, Official Bard of the Party, making use of quiet moments to compose more stanzas for the "Reso" song.)

The gradual reconstruction, now in last stages, has made possible larger living and dressing rooms—more suitably placed, improved dispensary and bathrooms (2), extra ward, jarrah-floored and gauzed-in verandahs. A new and commodious kitchen completes the establishment. Hearty thanks to all helpers!

The Club next door has been re-floored and improved generally, and a nice bathroom is now being fitted up for use of travellers. In the event of an epidemic, the Club will serve as an emergency ward.

THE HAMILTON.

The last flowing bore, 65 miles north of Oodnadatta, fills this pool on Stephenson River, just beside Mr. Harvey's famous "Do Drop In" store.

OODNADATTA-ALICE SPRINGS MAIL.

At Charlotte Waters Telegraph Station, a few miles north of the border between South and Central Australia. This station was built on "fort" lines in the early seventies to resist attacks from blacks. The walled-in courtyard remains, but old portholes were long since built in.

Afghan Crossing is remembered by all who pass by in dry times when one may have to "mat" the whole way. After rain one may do it on top gear.

mention a plunge or shower in the bathroom, which is just about to rise out of its former ashes into glories of enamel and paint.

From Oodnadatta the motor-mail (one large truck and a powerful car in use, S. Irvine, proprietor) leaves for Alice Springs on Sunday morning after train day—up there time is counted in fortnights rather than hours! The motor track goes via Hamilton Bore (66 miles) to Blood's Creek (100 miles) for the first night; on Monday it crosses the border into Central Australia seven miles before reaching the Charlotte Waters Telegraph Station (132 miles), and goes on via New Crown Point (cattle station, 150 miles), Old Crown Point store (177 miles), past Crown Point itself, a mile or so beyond, over Afghan Crossing on the Finke, to Horseshoe Bend (hotel, store, 'phone, cattle station—201 miles). Tuesday's run begins with two more crossings

Here we paused, while the wind blew sand around merrily, and put in a new crown wheel. Take your own garage with you always is the best policy in drought time up there.

over the Finke, followed by a third (Davis' Crossing, sometimes easy, sometimes beyond words), on over Dinny White's Crossing and the Hugh to Maryvale (cattle station 262 miles); from here the running is good to Deep Well (cattle station, 'phone, 284 miles), then fair to fine into Alice Springs (331 miles, 2,000 ft. above sea).

Every second trip the mail car goes out to Arltunga, 70 miles east; a run full of interest the whole way.

TAKE PLENTY OF MATTING ALSO.

IT PAYS TO JOIN FORCES CROSSING A STREAM.

The return journey begins the following Saturday, by the same stages, reaching Oodnadatta next Monday, with seven days clear before the train leaves. A margin is necessary, however, with ever-present risk of breakdown;

A humble effort to improve the Hugh River crossing—it helped what it didn't puncture.

Our motto in Central Australia is:
"Go while you can, stop when you must, but never worry!"

In this case, as usual, everything turned out rather simple. As the wheel had begun to break up 250 miles back, the mail driver just wired for a spare and "carried on" with over two tons to Alice Springs, something less to Arltunga, mail and passenger only for 18 miles of the return. A couple of hours after the final collapse, a Thursday afternoon, the A.I.M. wireless experimenters passed on way to Arltunga, so the mail party just "sat down" quietly till Saturday afternoon, when they would be given a lift back to Alice Springs.

Meantime, a wireless message was put through, telling the relief car not to worry. Mails and all turned up at Alice Springs safely on Saturday evening, and 12 hours behind time disappeared fast under the influence of night driving.

also for regular overhaul before the next trip which begins two days before the train leaves. Mails frequently catch a special train and thus save a week.

Central Australia has two additional mail services; one, by camel-pack, monthly, from Horseshoe Bend via Henbury to Hermannsburg—80 miles west of Alice Springs; the other, motor mail, every six weeks, goes north from Alice Springs via Ryan's Well (406 miles), Teatree Well (447 miles), Stirling Station (cattle, 484 miles), Barrow Creek (telegraph station, 504 miles), thence 100 miles to the border, and 180 miles through North Australia, via

This six-wheeler (with ten tyres) is merely amusing itself around Port Melbourne sand, with four tons of lead aboard. It expects to waltz all over Australia, eventually—while road-building is further discussed.

Tennant Creek telegraph station to Powell's Creek telegraph station. From Powell's Creek another motor-mail runs about 300 miles, every six weeks, to Emungalan

Eight hours of hard toil, just through turning off the track where the other fellow's track suggested an improved way. Sisters Small and Pope now claim to be expert road builders. They certainly earned their laurels. The car is "sitting down," supported on the treacherous ground by running-boards, etc.

(This gentleman is merely trying to find his wheel.)

It is fortunate that, sometimes, winds can resist temptation; but a northern motorman cannot turn away from any load.

After studying the preceding photographs, you will now be able to calculate the cost of this fodder for stud bulls at Arltunga in drought time—high price at Adelaide, 688 miles freight on rail, plus charges for 400 miles of what might best be termed "dead finish." Fortunately, the rain got there almost simultaneously with the first consignment.

(Katherine); unfortunately, it is not practicable to harmonise all timetables involved, so there is a dead spot in connections here.

Besides the mail cars, several motor trucks make regular trips north—proprietors, Wallis, Fogarty Ltd.

A word to intending motorists may be in season. Our references to difficulties must not be ignored, and our pictures tell their own stories; yet, somehow, practically all get through smiling. It must be remembered that rain, or a breakdown not imagined when spare parts were loaded up, may mean delay of anything up to a fortnight; but those have little sorrow who, amid rain and drought, practise these respective sayings: "Give the roads a chance to dry!" and "Mat early!" (i.e., put down the mats as soon as sand stops progress, instead of racing the engine and trying to jerk the car out of bottomless drift).

Ninety per cent. of the regular track offers no difficulty at all, and the rest is really bad only for limited periods.

"ROAD METAL."

Commissioner Stott deserves the honour conferred on him recently as Chief of Police in Central Australia. He is an enthusiast for spinifex crossings and new deviations, which promote good living even more than does fear of the law.

A ROAD-GANG AT WORK.

Under police direction, aborigines have occasionally done most useful work on the tracks. About 20 inches of spinifex, properly laid in the sand, is worth many times the trifling expense. Perhaps the main road across Australia will one day be esteemed worthy of a permanent party of road-menders!

YELLOW CLIFF.

At the exact "Geographical Centre" of Australia, just about two miles south of Crown Point; of special interest to geologists, because, embedded therein, may be found stones which have been "scored" by glacial action. They calculated that ice abounded all around only 270,000,000 years ago. Last summer, while replacing a broken axle in our car nearby, we calculated that the ice age was much further away than that!

Practically every type of car, from "Master" to "Baby," has gone through one time or another, also more than one omnibus, and all sorts of motor trucks.

AFGHAN CROSSING AND CROWN POINT.

CROWN POINT.

If in any doubt, write, or send reply-paid wire to the only emporium, "Wallis Fogarty Ltd., Oodnadatta, S.A." This firm has its branch store at Alice Springs, and a petrol dump at Tennant Creek. Its principals are keenly interested in local progress generally, as well as in their own business; their own drivers are continuously on the tracks.

FINKE RIVER, FROM CROWN POINT.

THE PROMISE OF A FINE SANDHILL.

We have not yet heard of their service-supply or advice as to condition of track letting anyone down.

Of the country passed through, starting from the railhead, the predominating features are "gibber" plains, i.e., vast stretches on which lie loose stones—mostly small and waterworn, but sometimes big and ugly—the residue of former, upper strata of conglomerate, long since eroded by the sport of wind and weather, except for die-hard patches like Crown Point. Belts of sand become more frequent

FINKE RIVER AT DAVIS' CROSSING.

DESERT OAKS.

OORAMINNA ROCKHOLE.

Three miles off the track, 30 miles south of Alice Springs; regarded by aborigines as a sacred spot, from which lubras are prohibited under pain of death. The lady motorist who is sitting on the bank—lately added, without success, in an attempt to conserve extra water—is counting up the blessings of white citizenship.

ON BURT PLAIN.

after passing Charlotte Waters, with spinifex thick upon the ridges between Old Crown and the open Emily Plain which provides a champion track for the last fifteen miles into Alice Springs. Seen in early morning, or at eventide, the panorama of Macdonnell Ranges, which opens out when one reaches this plain, is glorious.

Beyond these ranges, the forty-mile belt of Burt Plain —open saltbush and dense mulga alternately, with some

CENTRAL MOUNT STUART.
Close to the track 23 miles south of Barrow Creek.

ALICE SPRINGS.

(Officially termed "Stuart," this township has taken to itself the name of the telegraph station two miles north.)

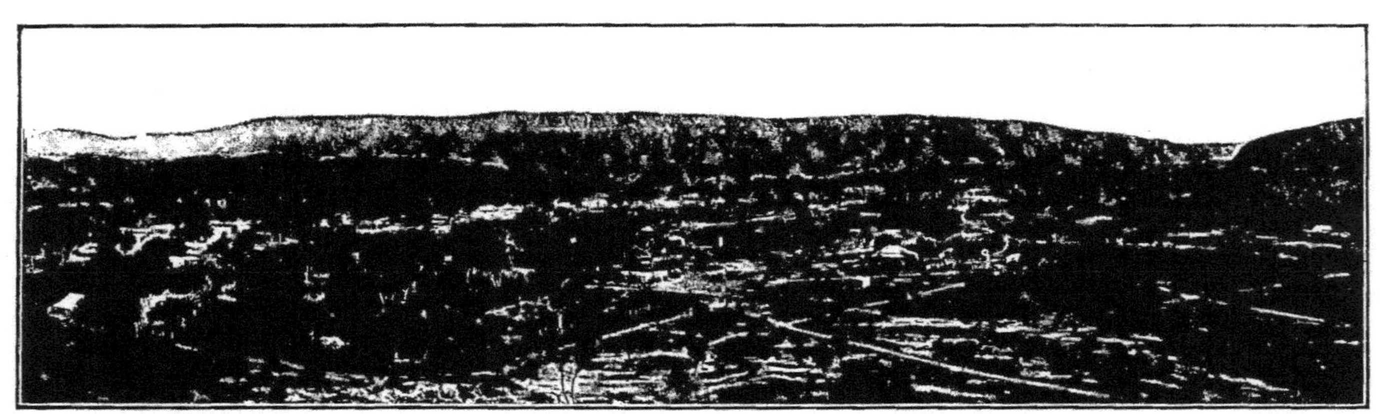

Store of Wallis Fogarty Ltd. — Mr. Ben Walkington's House. — Hotel behind trees. — The Bungalow — A.I.M. Home — Police Station — Home of Mr. Kramer. Missionary to Aborigines

Heavetree Gap, through which the railway will soon appear, may be seen in the right background. The station will be built on the clear space to the right foreground. The aerodrome lies close to the range on the right, just outside the picture.

BARROW CREEK'S BUSY DAY.

The "Reso Boys" so rushed the telegraph operator with farthest-north telegrams that he had no time to enjoy the occasion. It was at this lonely outpost, in 1874, that raiding blacks killed the staff—John L. Stapleton (operator), and John Franks (linesman). The hill is good company, but it served a bad purpose that day.

Mitchell grass—is a revelation in good seasons; beyond, shrubs of many kinds, with kangaroo grass and a type of spinifex that looks like a great wheatfield, makes the novice rush into dreams of the famous "potentialities." Much of this country is not so good as it looks by a long way; but, in places, traces of countless rabbits—that are not, now—indicate what maximum capacity sometimes is; but the local pastoralist, under present conditions of transport, must base all his calculations on minimum capacity!

Alice Springs, strictly speaking, signifies the telegraph station, two miles north of the township, just where the Todd River emerges from the hills; here, scour of flood waters against a rocky point keeps one spot washed out deep, leaving water—which is underlying everywhere near the bed—accessible to eye and bucket. Apparently, in the old days of 1872, when the O.T. line was put through, there were several such holes, hence the latter part of the name, which borrowed its first half from her who was afterwards known as Lady Todd—Sir Charles was leader of those stalwarts who "bullocked" the line through in the face of every imaginable difficulty. Mr. Allchurch, who also acts as magistrate, is in charge of this station, with three assist-

ALICE SPRINGS AND TODD RIVER.

ant operators, a battery man, and a linesman.

In the old days all cables for Australia came via Darwin and Alice Springs, and here every message had to be relayed by hand; now automatic machines do the work, but the staff at times find quite enough to do adjusting things to the moods of thunderstorms, or of the obsolete

HEAVETREE GAP.

Alice Spring's welcome to Col. Brindsmead, Controller of Civil Aviation, when on his way to meet Sir Alan Cobham.

primary batteries which are serving the instruments until the railway makes possible some modern electrical instalment—which, all hope, will include light, fans and refrigerators for the whole community. It may mean a change, bringing the post office into the township, just as historic "Katherine" station was closed in favour of Emungalan.

Meantime, the township has taken to itself the popular title, and uses its official name only when sending messages by 'phone from the store, to be relayed over the O.T. line.

GENERAL STORE, WALLIS FOGARTY LTD.

STUART ARMS HOTEL, ALICE SPRINGS.
The residential bungalow, recently added, may be seen in the background.

Business folk down south, never having heard of "Stuart," have a way of addressing the reply back to "Stuart's Creek," a railway siding already mentioned, between Marree and Oodnadatta. Southern papers, please copy!

Our pictures tell their own story as to facilities at Alice Springs, but mention must be made of the absence of a butcher in this metropolis of cattle country, though there is a saddler to handle leather. In season, a gardener

THE BALLROOM, ALICE SPRINGS.
Under the devoted hands of Mrs. Norman Jones, the canvas floor goes down, and the decoration "walls" rise up, whenever occasion demands.

"THE GARDEN."

One of the oldest homes in Alice Springs. Note the fine pepper trees. Once in business, but not now.

provides the most delightful watermelons and fine onions, with occasionally a few other lines. A bakery rises to the task when those who do not make their own bread bring along orders, and all the time keeps homely meals ready to cheer callers. A stock inspector, with his wife, lives just

These pepper trees rival weeping willows with their clinging foliage. They reach the underground waters.

SIMPSON'S GAP, 16 MILES WEST.

Many have visualised a big reservoir here, but the holding capacity of the ground has not yet been actually tested.

THE BUNGALOW, ALICE SPRINGS.

This temporary home for half-caste children has provoked many caustic comments, but its inmates exhibit more than ordinary happiness, and their self-discipline is beyond praise. Commodious new premises are about to be established on a reserve away from the town.

outside The Gap (Mr. and Mrs. Donald Campbell, who formerly presided over Ooenpelli, a beautiful aborigines' reserve in the extreme north of Northern Australia.

The school is still (temporarily since 1915) accommodated in rather cramped quarters kindly loaned by the Police Department, where Mrs. Standley gives her full share of service—teaching a few white children all morning, over 40 half-castes all afternoon, besides work as matron of the bungalow after school, and helping on all good works in her spare time. No wonder we all call her "Ma!"

Until last year, most of the nursing responsibilities fell to the kindly hands of Mrs. Stott and other ladies of the township, while Sergeant (now Commissioner) Stott drew teeth and set bones whenever need arose. Advice was often obtained by wire, with special medicine to follow a month or so later. For nearly a year, 1915-16, Sister Jean Finlayson represented the A.I.M.; but it became evident that a good building was essential, and early efforts to obtain the wherewithal were hindered by general depression.

MR. MEYER'S GRAPES, AT ALICE SPRINGS.

Then a big fete was held in Adelaide Town Hall, opened by Her Excellency Lady Helen Munro Ferguson, resulting in a useful nucleus fund. So a contract was placed with

HOW THE A.I.M. SISTERS CAME TO ALICE SPRINGS.

Some of our building timber came up by camel waggon, kindly lent by Sir Sidney Kidman, and some by camel pack.

the late Mr. Jack Williams—who also built the dam shown in our illustrations—to erect the substantial 18 inch stone walls. Working mostly single-handed, and burning his own lime, it was a tedious task indeed, but he built for the centuries.

Eventually Messrs. Bert and Angus McLeod arrived, with the A.I.M. Superintendent and Mr. Towns. Messrs. George Lewis and A. Sachse also served at different times; Sergeant Stott assisted in innumerable ways; some local aborigines, and others from Hermannsburg also lent a hand.

The rest came on motor lorries. This is a load! (Explanations in earlier pages.)

We burnt our own lime for plastering and odd masonry.

Owing to drought during our building operations, the horse waggon originally arranged for, by courtesy of the Hermannsburg Mission, could not take the field. So we carted in about 80 tons of ironwood logs in our devoted car.

The kiln was always too large when being charged, and too small when being emptied.

The service of McLeod brothers in keeping on against great handicaps was beyond praise. Fans and a share of the electrical equipment were given as a memorial to our young friend "Bill" Busby, of Wahroonga, N.S.W., whose early death crossed aspirations to serve eventually as an

IRONWOOD TREES.

This camel team is carting timber to burn lime for Government works.

By way of change, the car did an occasional ambulance trip The back of the seat was then removed.

An ambulance trip in wet weather (over 150 miles in chains), but really quite cosy—between stops! We travelled all through the second night, and reached Oodnadatta at 4.30 a.m., just with enough time for the Sisters there to prepare the patient for the long journey to Adelaide—train left at 7 a.m.

Bringing in raw material for reinforcing concrete—wire originally used to bind up camel-pack loads.

A.I.M. Padre. Some Adelaide friends supplemented this gift from parents who have thus, in some measure, fulfilled a lad's hopes; and our wireless friends, Messrs. Towns and Traeger, helped us out with the installation of the gear. Another "Bill," member of the Littlejohn clan of Scotch College fame, kindly keeps the gear in good form. We are grateful to Messrs. Shedden Adam and T. Darling, friendly architects of Sydney, for their patient help in working out so many varied ideas in the plans.

Twenty-seven A.I.M. enthusiasts came from Adelaide and Melbourne for the opening of the Home last year.

THE ADELAIDE HOME, ALICE SPRINGS.
Mount Gillan in background, 3,200 ft. above sea.

Last year, although the opening ceremony was somewhat premature, we had a great pilgrimage—27 A.I.M. enthusiasts from Melbourne and Adelaide, led by the Moderator-General, Rev. James Crookston; Conveners of our Inland Councils in Victoria and South Australia, Revs. J. A. Barber and D. A. Chapman, the veteran Convener and founder of the Smith of Dunesk Mission, Rev. Robert Mit-

SHOWING THE ENGINE ROOM.
Here extensive wireless experiments have been carried out; as a result, we hope, ere long, to instal a permanent transmitting station, which may enable our sisters to converse with a doctor far away, also to give advice to isolated residents within the district.

A noble bluff on Temple Bar Creek, six miles from Alice Springs. Note the unusual proximity of strata and conglomerate.

chell and Members of the House of Representatives, Messrs. Nelson, Stewart and Jackson.

So, at last in 1926, "The Adelaide Home"—hoped and worked for since 1913—became a reality, all gauzed in and furnished, which is quietly being enriched by Sisters Small and Pope. Messrs. Wilkinson and Adamson serve as Secretary and Treasurer, and residents are taking keen interest in developing a real haven for those who come in weak from illness and that subtle depression sometimes joined thereto—which we may call "bush shock." Our idea was a spot, in the very heart of the bush, where all might come at times **to forget that they are in the bush.** Our very love for the bush demands more retreats of this kind, which silently breathe their benediction.

Mention should be made of the kindly interest shown by those who pass by. The Resonians put up a record last month at a fete held under the leadership of the Govern-

You now know that Central Australia is not all sand! Neither is it all palms; so make the most of these, which abound in Palm Valley. The valley is about 15 miles south of Hersmannsburg mission, but, alas, can only be reached on horseback—and h o r s e s are seldom available!

JAY RIVER COUNTRY.

30 miles west of Alice Springs. The "New Bungalow" was started here, but exhaustive tests threw doubt on the water supply, and work was abandoned.

Picturesque cliffs adorn Palm Valley and guard the beauties therein.

P.S.—Ask why that motor track has not yet materialised.

(From Alice Springs to Hermannsburg, 80 miles west, the track is fair for cars; but there is no telephone to permit making arrangements with the mission people, even when horses might be within reach.)

THE DEVIL'S MARBLES.

A change in scenery where the track passes into "North Australia."

For several miles the track to Arltunga runs through Bitter Springs Gorge; the scenery is really unique for colourful rock, all blended with foliage.

ment Resident, Mr. T. C. Cawood, his wife and staff. The auctioneering boys from Horsham demonstrated a boomerang, which returned and returned until the sales clerk had registered £75—and yet some say you can get them for 2/- each! Then they tried fancy work, etc., which "boomeranged" almost as creditably, until the hard-working "Sisters"—staff and local ladies—were convinced that men were quite useful even at a needlework display.

Soon Alice Springs will have a "Council Chamber" to give visibility to the new status of Central Australia, also a Residency. We were glad to see two more windmills there since last year to lift the excellent well-water to thirsty gardens. A bowling-green must surely follow quickly, but we hope a worthy Inland Club will get there even earlier.

Space does not permit lengthy discussion of the resources of Central Australia. Mining is a closed book still, really, but evidence of gold, wolfram, mica, etc., guarantee

FOLDS IN THE ROCKS, ARLTUNGA TRACK.

that prospectors will be turning over the pages more eagerly after the railway makes serious development practicable. Lately we have had two types of prospector around in small numbers—some who have come, found, floated and sunk under difficulties; others have come, searched, and silently departed. We are wondering if they know something, and only wait till the chances of sinking are reduced to reasonable proportions.

THE POLICE STATION, ARLTUNGA.

Here, and at Hermannsburg, low-power wireless transmitters were set up last year during our A.I.M. experiments. Results, working in conjunction with "Central," were very promising, and we hope that a permanent service may ere long be realised.

Part of the White Range, Arltunga, an immense body of gold-bearing rock. It is low-grade, very hard, and would respond only to large-scale enterprise.

Agriculture, except to supply local needs, may be "forgotten" so far as this generation is concerned. Soil is good, water conservation may be possible; but without "snow storage," and with an evaporation rate of 7 feet 9 inches against irregular rainfall averaging only 11.1 inches, cost of large irrigation works would be prohibitive.

Pastoral resources are considerable, but very serious development of wells—artesian bores seem out of the question so far beyond and above all known basins—must be undertaken. The advice of Dr. Keith Ward to assist the development, in this respect, of **land already settled** is wise indeed.

Unfortunately, falls of rain are erratic as to season, and sudden, flooding storms in wrong months sometimes leave the country worse off than rain-gauge records would indicate.

Some years ago hundreds of men slaved on the Range, in twos and threes, gouging out the richer veins of ore for treatment at the Government Battery. Only memories remain. Miss Jack and Mr. D. S. Jackson, M.P., thinking out the future.

It must be confessed, also, that large areas are devoid of the right subsoil, which is a severe drawback. In this respect, the more arid lands around Oodnadatta are rather fortunate, as is evidenced by the presence of such semi-permanent waters as Hookey's Hole.

But the same objections must be laid against large areas of country in use elsewhere in Australia. We cannot afford to despise obvious values which remain.

The railway will lead to fenced paddocks, and sheep; use of small-supply wells which a cattleman sneers at, but quite useful when watched by boundary riders who go round on motor-cycles to look after engine pumps which keep up the supply for flocks of sheep.

2,000 CATTLE HEADING SOUTH.

Comparatively large areas must continue—not large areas for "big" men necessarily, but large areas for "small" men. Under present conditions, the latter remain poor even though some have runs comprising up to 1,000 square miles. The Hermannsburg Mission has 900 miles, but is not embarrassed with riches. None of the stations could

RAINFALL IN CENTRAL AUSTRALIA.

Oodnadatta, S.A., 125 miles south of border	Charlotte Waters 7 miles north of border	Alice Springs 160 miles (direct) north of border	Barrow Creek 160 miles (direct) north of A.S. 100 m. from N. bdr.	Hermannsburg 80 miles west of Alice Springs
ANNUAL AVERAGE FOR ABOUT 50 YEARS.				
4.8	5.4	11.1	12.1	9.1
RAINFALL PER YEAR FOR 15 CONSECUTIVE YEARS.				
4.9	3.2	7.7	11.1	6.5
2.6	2.4	5.4	3.9	4.1
5.4	9.6	15.9	14.1	10.9
8.9	3.7	13.1	38.8	8.0
3.4	3.9	9.5	3.8	5.3
3.1	2.1	12.0	8.9	6.8
6.4	5.4	9.8	9.5	7.3
8.5	12.3	17.6	8.9	15.7
2.9	2.7	8.0	13.5	7.8
8.1	6.8	18.2	15.7	13.4
3.5	4.8	7.0	7.0	7.9
2.1	2.7	8.9	10.4	9.4
6.1	4.3	8.4	13.4	6.5
4.3	9.0	10.5	10.6	17.1
1.8	1.4	4.3	7.9	2.2

HOMESTEAD AT LOVE'S CREEK STATION.

40 miles east of Alice Springs, the home of Mr. and Mrs. L. Bloomfield, both long identified with central pioneering. Mr. Bloomfield's interest has always been keen in horse-breeding; but motors, which are doing so much for the country in general, are not helping that. The station includes some excellent country.

DEFYING THE FLIES.

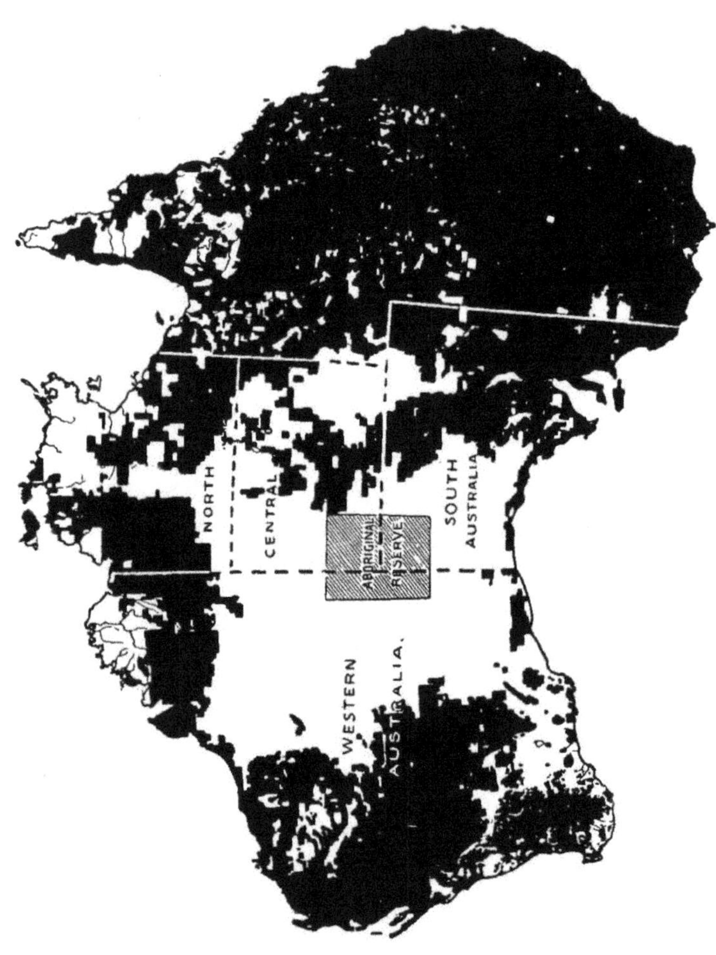

From a chart prepared by Dr. L. Keith Ward, showing—in black—Australia's lands already occupied under lease or freehold.

be called "gold-mines," though Crown Point, Henbury and Undoolya include 4,000, 4,000 and 2,500 sq. miles respectively.

Excluding that detached, occupied section of Central Australia which associates in commerce with Queensland, the figures for the zone of the coming railway are given as follow:—

46,458 square miles now occupied.
85,561 cattle.
15,010 horses.
9,801 goats.
6,093 sheep (mostly Arltunga way).
562 donkeys.
285 camels.
38 mules.
14 pigs.

For years past, with the railhead generally over 400 miles distant, sheep have been tried repeatedly in hope—and given up in despair—by men who are convinced that "small cattle" are normally the correct stock for their holdings.

Prime cattle, on the stations, mean medium to poor "stores" in the market. The railway may not pay, technically, but anything which increases the country's sum of wealth is worth while.

Speaking of lands, few realise the facts about "occupation" in this Continent. Both in North and Central Australia, approximately speaking, the areas occupied are equal, proportionately, to those of South and Western Australia.

Australia no longer has any "millions on millions of acres of fertile, virgin lands awaiting the settler." In Victoria, New South Wales and Queensland practically all the areas not reserved for national purposes are in use by pastoralists or agriculturalists. It is only by sane redistribution—insane subdivision, as proved in bitter experience, leads to reduced production, and failure all round—that good livings can be made possible for incoming settlers;

and such subdivision takes time, involving, generally, something expensive and tedious in multiplication of public works. That is why earnest men are apparently so slow in stimulating migration.

And reverting to the North-South railway, the missing section of which the Alice Springs extension is only a forty per cent. instalment. It will have a wonderful value which cannot be computed in terms of £ s. d.; for it will make it easier for us to give the lie—rather the revelation or "showdown"—to those dreamers who patter about us Australians as idle dogs in a rich, meat-filled manger. That will be something in these days of a League of Nations which, every day and in every way, grows better and better at minding everybody's business.

Since the preceding paragraph was first penned, the morning paper has quoted our own British spokesman, Sir Austen Chamberlain, confessing his faith as follows:—

> **"The judgment of the League is the judgment of the highest tribunal before which, here on earth, any nation can appear to justify its action, and of whose approval any nation will have infinite need in a moment of trial and trouble."**

We Australians who, lightheartedly, for four generations, have been reading to Aborigines the "move aside clause," will surely be called up to render an account of our stewardship—God only knows how soon. Those who really inspect the frontiers of settlement in this weird land know that only with a great sum of travail do we obtain our heritage—and the sweaty price is far from paid in full, and the rich rewards are yet a long way off. The building of our railway to Central Australia will lead to a multiplication of those qualified to tell the facts to the world, instead of belching out ninety per cent. imaginative trash which may be used—though erroneous, yet "out of our own mouth"—to condemn ourselves.

These parts are an asset, out of which we can earn profits; **and we will earn all we get!**

DAM, BOND SPRINGS (16 MILES NORTH-EAST).

It is well to remember—while planning out the wonderful things to be done by bright young pioneers soon to "show how"—that much costly endeavour has been put forth in the past. Wells and dams (including "duds") have cost money and effort, of which, we fear, no adequate record is available. Systematic development, not all at cost of leaseholders, will repay the nation in due course.

The embankment is of masonry, but some seepage will be noticed from under the foundations.

THE "RESO" CAMP AT ALICE SPRINGS, AUGUST, 1927.

CAPTAIN BAGOT'S FIRST PARTY OF TOURISTS.

We would like to tell something of the efforts of Captain Bagot and others who, we strongly suspect, earned much more than they got in trying to stimulate a flow of opened-eyed Australians across the Continent.

And we would like to put in a whole article on the "Reso" (resources) Party, led by Mr. C. H. Holmes (of the Betterment and Publicity Board, Victorian Railways), to Barrow Creek and back—in which the A.I.M. Superintendent had a place. The sixty members of this party (apart from thirty mechanics and attendants) were not "tourists," but representative citizens, leaders in all kinds of undertakings—commercial, mining, manufacturing, agricultural, pastoral, research, medicine, public welfare and journalism. Chief Commissioner Clapp had given much personal attention to the enterprise, not as a mere railway matter so much as a National Gesture of Southern interest in the Centre of our National Home. To be sure, all travelled like so many schoolboys; and that, after all, is all the best statesmen can hope to be—young enough to remain happy, and always picking up fresh ideas to work off on the boys left at home!

But our space is long since exhausted, and we dare not ask for yet another extension. So you must seek out your friend who went up with the "Reso" or some other party, and get enough further particulars to make you start

EVIDENCE OF "RESO" ORGANISATION!

THE SECRET OF RESONIANS' GOOD HUMOUR.

This champion "cooker" was folded up every morning and loaded on the motor lorry. Within 20 minutes after reaching evening camp, it would be set up and have pots simmering.

Evening dress, as worn among Australia's oldest families on State occasions.

your own personal "Travelling Fund" to see Australia before you set out to tell the world.

All visitors seem to be well pleased with the climate—most take care to come during the cooler months—and the scenery. Of the latter, much is really splendid; as to the rest, it is so "different" to the eyes of those from the south-east that it is often reckoned even more interesting than scenery proper. They love the clear air of our cheery warm days—accentuated by night "zero" hours of anything down to 23 degrees!

The Resonians were fortunate in their "Motor Captain," Mr. Murray Aunger, who was, in company with Mr. Dutton, the first to motor across the Continent via Central Australia. They set out in November, 1906, battled across the plains, sand ridges and hills, through bogs, wash-outs and tall grass—one day doing eleven miles by hurrying

GETTING UP PACE TO RUSH DEPOT SANDHILLS.

Mr. Murray Aunger (at the wheel), and many others, have gone over the very worst sand by using these "sand-grips." On the front wheels the steel bars—which support a leather belt on each side of the tyre—are clearly seen. Latterly, deviations of the track around bad patches have eliminated this need for ordinary travel. The notorious Depot Sandhills lie just north of Horseshoe Bend—but now the track goes round, as motorists prefer to do over 20 miles extra to avoid trouble.

from daylight till dark—broke down somewhere beyond Alice Springs on Xmas eve, and came home without the car. Next July they set out again from Adelaide in a second car, and won through to Darwin, recovering the first car on the way, in 42 days. Judging by the 100 miles covered by Mr. Aunger on this trip in 3 hours 10 minutes, he will cross next time in 4 days! The Resonians left Melbourne after lunch on August 2nd, travelled by train to Oodnadatta, and motor to Barrow Creek; never hurrying, spending two nights at Alice Springs each way; and were back in Melbourne just after lunch on August 18th.

Times are changing!
Watch them change!
Change them right!

1. JOHN FLYNN AT THE GRAVE OF "SCRUB BULL" (DUNCAN McCAULEY)
2. GORDON DOWNS HOMESTEAD, EAST KIMBERLEY
3. HOMESTEAD ON A CATTLE STATION IN THE KIMBERLEYS

TYPICAL A.I.M. NURSING HOMES

1. SISTER KING ON HER WAY TO WIMMERA NURSING HOME, VICTORIA RIVER DOWNS

2 and 3. SCENES ON THE KATHERINE RIVER

INLAND PIONEERS

1. BOAB, OR BOTTLE TREE, NORTHERN AUSTRALIA
2. DESERT COUNTRY AFTER RAIN
3. BANYAN TREE, NORTHERN AUSTRALIA

1 and 2. ANT HILLS IN THE NORTHERN TERRITORY
3. "MOTOR GRID," OR BY-PASS, PASSABLE FOR CARS, BUT NOT FOR STOCK

DONKEY AND CAMEL TEAMS

MUSTERING CATTLE

HISTORY OF THE MOVEMENT A word as to history of this important venture may be of interest. Having begun to help solve the medical problems of the frontiers by placing nursing sisters out in the isolation, the A.I.M. was concerned because many cases called urgently for advice from a doctor. Yet, in certain sections, resident doctors could never be supported by such scanty population; and, even if salaries were forthcoming, there would not be sufficient "practice" to keep them in form. Even if a doctor could be stationed at every Nursing Home now established, there would be many pioneers beyond reach within reasonable time.

By 1917, we were satisfied that aeroplanes and wireless were the only possible solution. In 1918 we published a fine article from the pen of the late Clifford Peel, a young medical student from Inverleigh, Victoria, who had joined the A.F.C. He wrote this article—setting out the practicability of Flying Doctors—while on the transport, and had given his life in France before it actually appeared in print.

Much discussion followed, and throughout all the years since then the Press of Australia has generously given wonderful aid in spreading the idea. For their persistence in reiterating the facts, we are deeply grateful.

Mr. C. Alma Baker, who had done so much to inspire gifts of fifty battleplanes from private citizens to the A.F.C., talked enthusiastically with us about the possibilities, and from him we received a cheering letter in June, 1919:—

> "The brave pioneers living in these practically uninhabited parts are now entirely cut off from doctors and nurses. None but the men, women and children who live in the Never-Never can appreciate the great blessing and boon an aerial medical service will be to them.
>
> "The people of the Never-Never are the people who help to keep the big commercial centres together, and those who live in big cities and towns of Australia must realise what these men outback have done, and are doing, for the business of the community.

"I think you will find no difficulty, when you eventually launch your scheme for subscriptions for your aerial service, in getting the commercial communities of Australia, as well as the big pastoralists and others, to help finance you in this very laudable proposition; and on my return to Sydney, at the end of July, I will have much pleasure in giving you £100 towards your aerial medical service."

In due course Mr. Baker's donation was placed in a separate fund, which grew very slowly year by year. That fund enabled us to initiate our wireless experiments in 1925.

Meantime, the late Mr. H. V. McKay had entered into the discussion, and, by way of hastening preliminaries, had assisted materially in promoting Western Australian Airways, Ltd. He and the A.I.M. Superintendent were strongly of the opinion that an actual start would not be advisable until aerial mails were strongly established, and that the new service should be based on their organisations. So we all kept on sowing ideas in hope, meantime.

Mr. McKay was specially interested because the Editor of "The Inlander" used to work ferrets in stone walls fast being displaced by the homes of his employees; and he was planning to assist in launching a vigorous appeal when, all unexpectedly, a health trip abroad became imperative.

That effort to stave off his own trouble proved futile; but, on his return, Mr. McKay immediately gave attention to our old dream—and more. The great Charitable Trust (which will not function in full strength for some time) was then wrought out; it will stimulate all kinds of national welfare enterprises, particularly those in the interests of remote pioneers.

Soon after Mr. McKay's death, the Trustees entered into consultation with the A.I.M., and offered £2,000 towards an experiment, provided that adequate support was given in other quarters. Last September, the General Assembly of Australia authorised the A.I.M. Board to take all necessary steps towards consumation of this long-cherished ideal.

Our special Aerial Ambulance Committee was then constituted, and the Wool Brokers' Association entered into the Campaign. As already stated, many patriots have quietly hastened to join in. In due course the Commonwealth and Queensland Governments gave their benedication, and success now seems within reach.

Last June, our Victorian Chairman, Rev. J. Andrew Barber, B.A., on whom had fallen much of the burden of organising support for the A.M.S., set out on a long investigation of the interior. With him went Dr. George Simpson, who is now Hon. Secretary for our special A.M.S. Committee

They motored from Adelaide, via Port Augusta, to Coober Pedy Opal Fields, across to William Creek, and on through Oodnadatta, Alice Springs, and Marranboy to Darwin; then to Victoria River country, and back to Marranboy; then to Barkly Tableland, where they talked over matters with many, including the amateurs who operate the Brunette Downs wireless station; then via Camooweal and Mt. Isa to Cloncurry.

At Cloncurry the A.M.S. proposal was very widely discussed. It so happened that, amid it all, a call came from Mt. Isa for Qantas to send an aeroplane to bring in a patient suffering from a broken pelvis—rather a grave injury. Dr. Simpson went with the 'plane, after making preparations, watched over the patient during the return flight, and handed him over to Cloncurry hospital none the worse for the journey.

This case is interesting as showing the interdependence of various units in the inland medical army. The doctor at Mt. Isa had not sufficient facilities to care for such a case, so had to arrange for a transfer; the aeroplane could not land closer than a mile and a half from the spot where the patient lay, so the Q.A.T.B. motor ambulance had to be called in; the roads were so rough, and the patient's injury so critical, that that mere mile-and-a-half seemed more than enough—they could never have attempted 150 miles of round-about tracks to Cloncurry.

PREPARING TO START FROM MT. ISA.

the 'plane could not land anywhere near the Cloncurry hospital, so another Q.A.T.B. motor ambulance was waiting at the aerodrome to serve over the last, short lap.

Incidently, this journey provided an emphatic demonstration of two facts already accepted by our promotors. First, a doctor is required to accompany serious cases on their flight; second, the mail aeroplanes—the actual machine illustrated in our photographs will be in use, turn about, during the experimental year of our A.M.S.—are admirably suited for ambulance service, merely needing the addition of temporary rests for the stretcher.

Resuming their journey, our investigators motored on to Boulia and Birdsville, then doubled back via Betoota to Longreach.

Last month a definite date was fixed for a start of operations, 1st April, of next year—by which time the wet season should be over, and all preparations complete.

To all who have battled for this "Mantle of Safety" to spread over isolated pioneers we tender our sincerest gratitude. The memory of those departed colleagues is with us as we turn to great realities—which their faith has brought so near. Complete fulfilment may not come quickly—as children count time—but there should be no further pause.

This photo was taken at Cloncurry by Rev. J. A. Barber. The patient with a broken back is still in the 'plane, after travelling 125 miles by air. Centre, Dr. Simpson; right, Captain Evans (pilot); left, Q.A.T.B. Officer. This actual 'plane (D.H. 50) will be used alternately with others of the same type throughout the Aerial Medical Service experimental year.

THE CHIEF VIRTUE. Once more we would emphasise the special value of such a boon as an Aerial Medical Service throughout our uniquely-lonely frontiers. To heal the sick? No!

There will be sick folk, young and old—all too many. And there will inevitably be terrible accidents, for man seems to be born thereto. At such times the value of the A.M.S. will be obvious to all.

But the chief virtue will not be that; it will be, in the hearts of our Australian people, a sense of security—so far as mortal man or woman can expect or desire. With no physical hurt actually present, women out there will be able to reject the little, unseen imps that keep on jeering "What would happen if. . . ?

The A.M.S. will eliminate that old, old dread! And eliminate it also from hearts of many mothers, and sisters, and wives-elect who remain in cities themselves, while their loved ones work far, far beyond the sunset. And happy homes "furnished with children" will become more numerous in our lands of loneliness.

Yes. Even if it could eventuate that frontier Flying Doctors should be "idle" most of the time, we know that, all the time, they would be infusing new life into the alleged "dead heart" of this continent.

Our supreme concern is with the spirit of man. The A.M.S. will be a wonderful Sacrament of Comradeship, revealing the essential unity of our busiest cities and our emptiest provinces! Write in your hearts this great spiritual significance of our forthcoming enterprise; and, if future A.M.S. doctors are not run off their feathers, say "God be praised!" And tell them to keep on standing by, proud to be incorporated in the ever-enlarging flame rekindled by our "Lady with a Lamp."

AN EXPERT'S POINT OF VIEW.

NOTE: Dr. George Simpson has prepared a report for his professional brethren—who are naturally very much interested. Portion of that report, hereunder, should be studied with care by all concerned.

Dr. Simpson grew up on a station well known to cattle men for its stud stock; one of his brothers was an "Ace" in the A.F.C.; he has watched and worked for the Inland ever since he could read about it; in 1925 he took an active part in preparations for A.I.M. wireless experiments, and spent some time around Beltana; later, in London, he discussed the proposed A.M.S. with many enthusiasts, including some of those silent men who had taken part in military aerial ambulance services in arid countries "somewhere in or around the British Empire." Lastly, as already related, he investigated conditions within and beyond our first A.M.S. district, and now he assists as Hon. Secretary of the special Committee in Melbourne.

It is expected that one Doctor may be able to operate over a 300 mile radius; and therefore, theoretically, six flying Doctors would practically cover the whole Inland. It is proposed to operate in conjunction with existing aerial mail services.

to supply their medical needs. They have been looking to the A.I.M. to commence an aerial service, which they will welcome and wholeheartedly support.

Air travel in the Cloncurry area is no novelty. It is accepted as is road travel in other parts. Patients are continually being brought to hospital by the air services, but of course it is at cost which only a few can afford.

Three schemes for supplying aerial medical services were considered.

(1) Aerial ambulance pure and simple, run on ordinary ambulance lines without a medical attendant.

(2) Machine specially fitted as an ambulance owned an operated by the A.I.M. and to carry a doctor.

(3) Machine adapted as an ambulance to carry doctor and patient, operated for the A.I.M. by contract with an air service at present working.

From the small available data it seems essential for a medical man to fly with the machine, for:—

(1) In most cases, no medical man will have seen the case before arrival of the ambulance. It will be necessary for a provisional diagnosis to be made; for first aid treatment to be rendered; and the advisability of air transport to be decided on. The pilot would receive instructions for making the trip satisfactory, and comfortable, for the particular case. He would be advised as to the best altitude—whether to avoid (if possible) bumping, vibration, etc.

First aid treatment would include special preparation for transport, injection of Morphia, etc.

(2) Treatment may be needed during the flight. In case of air-sickness and vomiting it may be necessary to clear mouth. Injection of Morphia may be needed in accident cases. Stimulants may be needed. Adjustments of splints, etc., may be necessary.

(3) In exceptional cases a forced landing may be advisable. This decision could only be made by a competent observer, and the Pilot should not be asked to land unless absolutely essential.

(4) The Pilot has his own responsibilities, and should not be expected to have any worry from his passengers.

The medical attendant takes all responsibility of the patient.

For the above and other reasons it is considered essential that a medical man fly with the aeroplane, and return with the patient. This means that the first scheme would not be satisfactory.

As regards the second scheme—machine owned by A.I.M. : A single machine, without an organisation, would be practically useless in the inland regions or Australia. For this reason the scheme cannot be considered; therefore the third alternative is the only one likely to work. The scheme will present many difficulties; but I am convinced, as a result of investigation in the area, that it is quite practicable.

"It will be impossible to formulate a code of rules and arrangements for the working of the scheme until it is actually in operation. It must necessarily be experimental at first; rules first made will be broken, and changed, and gradually a working organisation may be evolved which will, later, be applicable to other centres.

There will be the difficulty of communication, for the call must first come to the doctor, and rapid communication is the first essential to an efficient medical service.

There is a skeleton telegraph and telephone system throughout the Cloncurry area. There are wires as far west as Avon Downs, and as far south as Boulia and Urandangi, and north to Normanton and Burketown. Brunette Downs has wireless.

For the most part the stations are completely isolated, and it is in the development of wireless that the possibilities are greatest. Recent experiments carried on by the A.I.M. have proved that a cheap, reliable, short-distance set can be produced. It is hoped, by establishing these at strategic centres in touch with a central station, to supply communication to the whole area.

The possibilities of using carrier pigeons might also be considered for urgent messages. This method is used in parts of the Inland. It seems essential to first develop communication, but useful calls will come from the present system. Still, the object of the scheme should be always to get beyond the existing systems; to supply a medical service to people at present having none, not to better a service which may at present be quite good.

There are many problems connected with the working of the 'plane. These have been solved by Qantas (Queensland and Northern Territory Aerial Services Ltd.), which has the highest efficiency record, and whose 'planes fly about 40,000 miles a month in Queensland. It will be necessary to establish new landing grounds, so that every home can be reached, but ready co-operation of the local residents will make this an easy task.

For efficiency of service and organisation, Qantas is the ideal service to supply the 'plane, under the contract which has been proposed, viz.:—

> "That they have continuously available, at Cloncurry, one 'plane fitted as an ambulance, for the use of A.I.M. Doctor" is very sound.

The D.H. 50 machine is a standard type with Qantas, and it is practically ideal as an ambulance. The cabin is easy of access. It is long enough to carry a stretcher case, and wide enough to allow attendant to be beside the patient, and to attend to him. Its flying performance is fine, and the special type of undercarriage renders landing particularly free from bumping. There is also easy means of communication between pilot and the doctor in charge of the case.

The question of overlapping of existing medical and ambulance services has been considered. The medical men in the area are all subsidised by hospital committees, and have little private practice. They are all isolated, and, in every case, said they would welcome a "flying doctor" who would be available for consultations and for anaesthetics, etc.

The motor ambulance is generally accepted as being chiefly useful for distances under 50 miles. The usefulness of the 'plane would commence at 50 miles, so there could be no question of overlap. We found the local ambulance authorities enthusiastic supporters of the scheme.

The flying range has been set down at 250-300 miles, greater distances being possible in special cases.

Cloncurry is most suitable as a base because of the hospital, and being the 'plane base. Qantas, at present, have always a spare 'plane and pilot at Cloncurry; this would be kept exclusively for the aerial medical service, but not necessarily always the same 'plane, thereby allowing periodic overhaul without interruption.

The object of the experiment is to demonstrate that, by means of air transport, a doctor can extend his services over the flying range. Therefore it is suggested that his work be:—

(1) To attend urgent and accident cases—render first aid treatment, and, if advisable, transport by air to the nearest suitable hospital, where the case will be transferred entirely to the local staff.

(2) To pay regular visits to places at present entirely outside the medical area for the purpose of attending more chronic cases.

(3) To be available, when desired, for consultations with local doctors.

The A.I.M. medical man will be subsidised by the A.I.M., and will personally receive no fees. He will have no private practice. The actual working of the scheme will be controlled by a local committee, acting under direction of the A.I.M. Board.

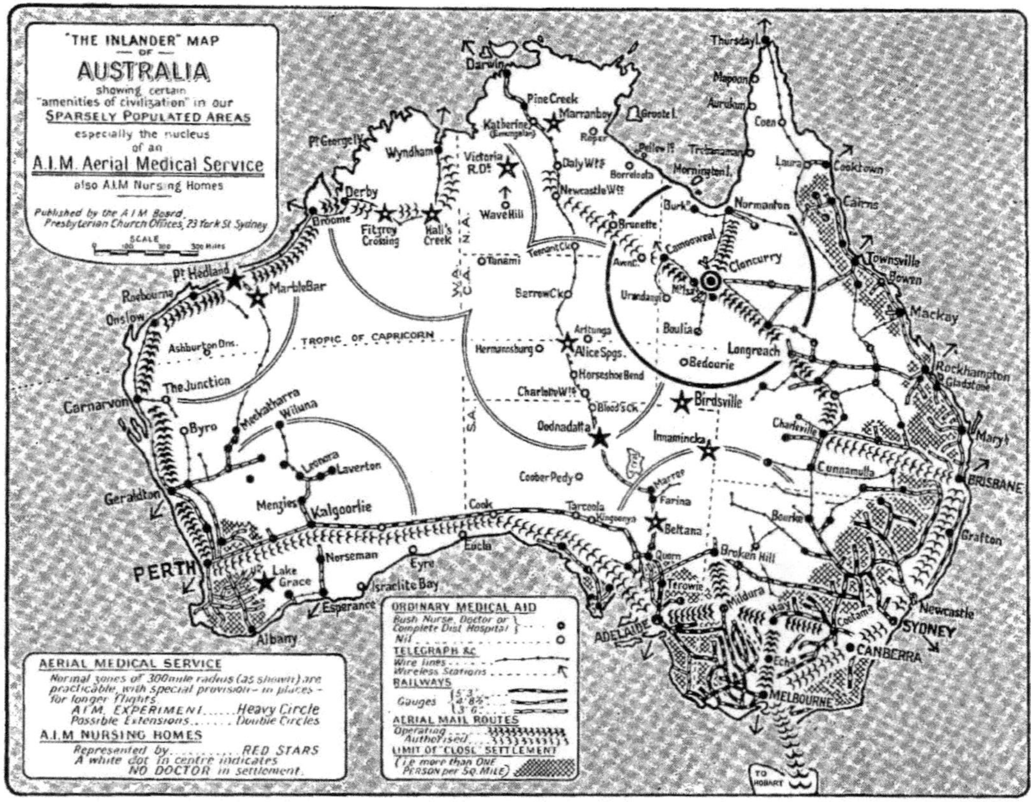

Fitzroy Crossing and Innamincka Nursing Homes are not yet completed, but contracts have been arranged.

All interested in the A.I.M. are urged to secure a copy of this map, in larger size 10 in x 7½ in., in colours, and to hang it on their wall for reference.

Blocks and Map.
A. A. Lawson Ltd.

1 and 2. JERVOIS RANGE, CENTRAL AUSTRALIA
3. CROWN POINT, CENTRAL AUSTRALIA

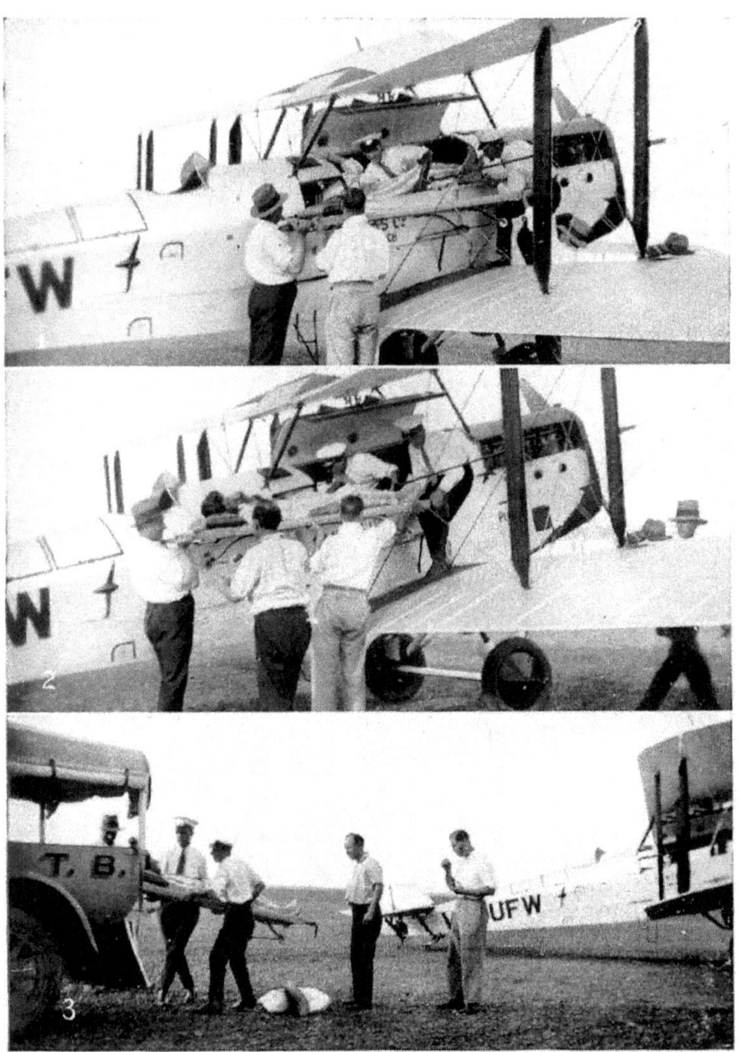

THE AERIAL MEDICAL SERVICE IN ACTION

1. MOOLABULLA GOVERNMENT CATTLE STATION
2. TEMPORARY HOMESTEAD, EAST KIMBERLEY
3. KANGAROO GRASS COUNTRY, NORTHERN AUSTRALIA

1. BRUNETTE DOWNS HOMESTEAD
2. POLICE STATION, WAVE HILL
3. OPENING OF WAVE HILL WIRELESS STATION

1. ROYAL HOTEL, BEDOURIE
2. BEDOURIE BORE. DAILY OUTPUT 1,250,000 GALLONS
3. BOULIA, QUEENSLAND

1. OLD HOME IN ALICE SPRINGS, CENTRAL AUSTRALIA
2. TRAEGER AND HIS BABY WIRELESS TRANSMITTER

1. A DUG-OUT COOBER PEDY OPAL FIELD
2. A CAMEL RIDER
3. PIONEER HOMESTEAD

www.ingramcontent.com/pod-product-compliance
Ingram Content Group Australia Pty Ltd
76 Discovery Rd, Dandenong South VIC 3175, AU
AUHW010912290126
422696AU00005B/8

9 781923 52705